CYC
CLIMBS OF
NORTH-EAST
ENGLAND

A ROAD CYCLIST'S GUIDE

SIMON WARREN

F

FRANCES
LINCOLN

Cycling Climbs of North-East England: A Road Cyclist's Guide
© 2017 Quarto Publishing plc.
Text, photographs, design and illustrations © Simon Warren, 2017

First Published in 2017 by Frances Lincoln,
an imprint of The Quarto Group.
The Old Brewery, 6 Blundell Street,
London N7 9BH, United Kingdom.
www.QuartoKnows.com

All rights reserved.
No part of this publication may be reproduced, stored in a
retrieval system, or transmitted, in any form, or by any means,
electronic, mechanical, photocopying, recording or otherwise
without the prior written permission of the publisher or a licence
permitting restricted copying. In the United Kingdom such licences
are issued by the Copyright Licensing Agency, Barnards Inn,
86 Fetter Lane, London EC4A 1EN

A catalogue record for this book is available from the British Library.

978-0-7112-3705-6

Printed and bound in China

1 2 3 4 5 6 7 8 9

Brimming with creative inspiration, how-to projects and useful information to enrich
your everyday life, Quarto Knows is a favourite destination for those pursing their
interests and passions. Visit our site and dig deeper with our books into your area of
interest: Quarto Creates, Quarto Cooks, Quarto Homes, Quarto Lives, Quarto Drives,
Quarto Explores, Quarto Gifts, or Quarto Kids.

Thanks to my family and friends for their endless support
and patience, as always. Thanks to my Dad, who accompanied me on my
research trips and took control of the car when my back went pop.
And finally thanks to all the Strava users and Twitter followers who
suggested climbs for me to seek out, especially David Alexander
for his expert guidance on the hills of County Durham.

Disclaimer: This book reports information and opinions which may be of general interest
to the reader. Neither the author nor the publisher can accept responsibility for any accident,
injury or damage that results from using the ideas, information or advice offered in this book.

CONTENTS

The Cheviot Hills

NORTHUMBERLAND

NEWCASTLE
UPON TYNE

The Pennines

COUNTY
DURHAM

TEESSIDE

THE NORTH-EAST

I somewhat overlooked the North-East of England when I wrote *100 Greatest Cycling Climbs*, for a couple of what I thought were legitimate reasons. Firstly, the list I had was filling up very fast with climbs from other areas, and secondly, there just weren't enough of what I considered 'famous' hills that needed to be included. I tried to make amends in *Another 100 Greatest Cycling Climbs*, but I still only scratched the surface, so I was eager to go back and have a proper look around for this volume.

As you flick through the pages of this book you will see plenty of snow, and these pictures were all taken on one of the best days I have ever had on the bike. It was early February 2012 and freezing cold; the hills were covered with a substantial dusting of snow and yet, miraculously, the roads were clear. There was no ice, no slipping, no danger, and the contrast of the grey tarmac against the white backdrop was just fantastic. I'd say those sort of conditions are almost perfect for the Weardale landscape, as they accentuate the wild and remote nature of the barren hills.

To finish my research, I had actually planned one long trip towards the end of summer 2016, but unfortunately, things didn't quite go to plan. I had been experiencing some back pain over the summer but just put up with it, as you do. I thought back pain was for old people, so I simply refused to listen my body and chose to ride though the discomfort. And anyway, it only really hurt when I did more than four hours on the bike, and I could live with that... But on day one of this trip it hurt just that little bit more than usual; of course a long drive never helps, so I pushed on. My dad had come along for the journey to help with the driving; he was enjoying our father-son trips, and

we arranged a meeting point so he could go bird watching while I ticked off the first few climbs. We met up as planned, I moaned a bit about the pain, and we split up again. Then, with two climbs to go, after stopping to take pictures on White Edge (page 50), I remounted the bike and BANG. Perhaps it wasn't a bang, but it was a cracking noise of some sort, and that was it – I was stuck in an upright position, and my back bloody hurt. Unsurprisingly there was no phone signal on the hill, but thankfully my dad was due to meet me again just over the brow – I just had to reach him. I somehow managed to ride the bike out of the saddle, almost standing straight up, drag my broken body to the top of the climb, and freewheel down the other side. I stopped

for a while, managed to stretch a bit, and decided I would try to keep going, because NOTHING stops me. But no, it was game over. Damn. We got back to the hotel and I had to make the tough decision to cancel the next day. I knew I'd hurt something properly this time, so there was no choice but to call off the trip and get fixed up. Thank heavens I hadn't travelled alone – Dad drove all the way back while I sought help for my back on Twitter. Thankfully, I got it fixed: just a single session with an osteopath followed by a trip to a brilliant sports physio at Cyclefit in Covent Garden and I was as good as new. And also armed with some advice on stretching and general body maintenance to prevent a repeat. With hotels rebooked, it was time to head north to finish the job,

this time solo. It was now quite late in the year, but I got very lucky with the weather for the most part and had a couple of great days riding in Northumberland. I travelled back through County Durham to finish off with an afternoon on Teesside.

It was during this trip that I found my new favourite north-eastern climb, Prospect Hill (page 92). I hate it when I discover a climb that I had no idea existed because I feel like I've missed out, but at the same time I also love it – it's like finding an extra present late on Christmas Day. And if anything it's a good thing to be constantly surprised by new and wonderful roads. Maybe there are still some killer hills in these parts I've yet to find – in fact, I hope there are.

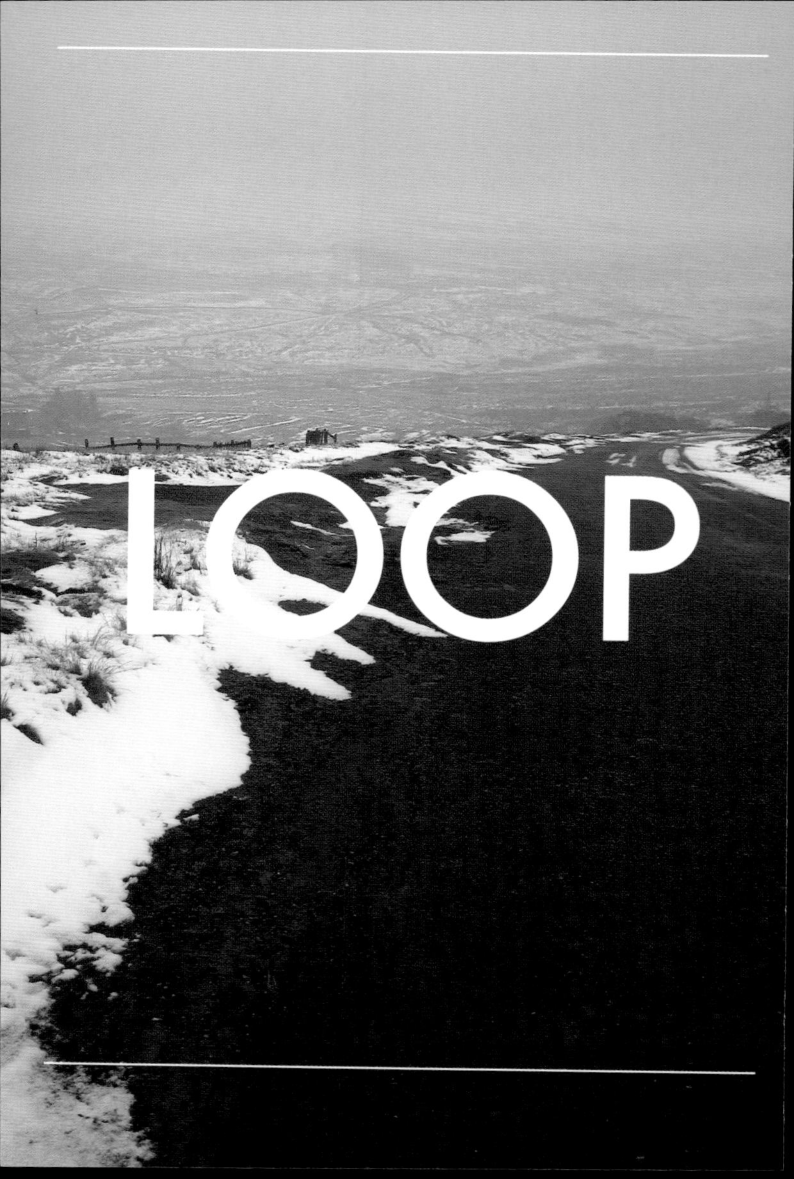

LOOP

When I plan a ride, whether it's for research or leisure (which my wife will tell you are both the same), I always endeavour to build the route into one simple loop. The aim when plotting is to include as many climbs as possible without backtracking or using the same road twice. This isn't always feasible, but when I achieve it, there's always a great sense of satisfaction.

To experience the best of County Durham you couldn't do much better than to ride this relatively short yet challenging loop from Saint John's Chapel. Taking in six of the climbs in this book, and descending a further three, it's fair to say it's a hilly ride: 1,700 metres of altitude gained over 74 kilometres.

Leaving Saint John's Chapel you have a brief warm-up before you hit the first and toughest climb on the route, Peat Hill (page 64). Its 25% bends writhe out of Westgate and lead you away from the sanctuary of Weardale and up to Scarsdale Head. You next plunge down to cross Rookhope Burn and tackle Cuthbert's Hill (page 60). Almost as tough as Peat Hill, it deliver you via its fantastic curves to the solitude of the empty moorland. Then you begin your circumnavigation of Stanhope Common. Descending towards Blanchland you can divert left into the village if you need supplies, or turn right to climb Bale Hill (page 46). After a long descent the early slopes will hurt your legs, but there's also a substantial respite on this climb. Heading south, you descend Crawleyside (page 66) into Stanhope before wrestling the savage twin hairpins of Unthank Bank (page 68), climbing immediately back out of Weardale. Now comes the best part of the ride: the majestic Bollihope Common (page 72). Following a short descent into the gully at its base, the journey to the top of this climb is phenomenal. Never too steep (apart from the very first corner) but a stiff challenge nonetheless.

There's a long drop down into Middleton-in-Teesdale and a brief stint on the B6282, then it's time for the final ascent up Newbiggin Common (page 74). Long and arduous, this should be enough to finish you off for the day. But if you still have fresh legs once back in Saint John's Chapel, head south to tick off the brutal Chapel Fell (page 56).

Blanchland

BALE HILL

CUTHBERT'S HILL

STANHOPE COMMON
Rookhope

B6278

PEAT HILL

ST JOHN'S CHAPEL
START/FINISH

Westgate

A689

Stanhope

UNTHANK BANK

BOLLIHOPE COMMON

NEWBIGGIN COMMON

MIDDLETON COMMON

B6282
Newbiggin

Middleton-in-Teesdale

B6278

B6282

REMEMBER
to check
your bike, check
your body, wear
a helmet, and, above
all, have fun!

LEGEND

LOCATIONS

You will be able to locate each hill from the small maps provided: simply, **S** marks the start and **F** marks the finish. I would suggest you invest in either Ordnance Survey maps or a GPS system to help plan your routes in more detail. The grid reference in the Factfile locates the summit of each climb, and in brackets is the relevant **OS Landranger** map. The graphic at the start of each chapter will show you where the hills lie in the context of each region.

TIMINGS

Each Factfile includes the approximate time needed to ride each hill. Timed over the distance marked, this is how long it took me to complete each climb at a reasonable, but comfortable pace. Since I rode in all weathers, from blizzards to baking heat, I have adjusted the times slightly to accommodate for the adverse conditions I faced on the day. The times could be used as a target but are really just intended to help you plan your rides.

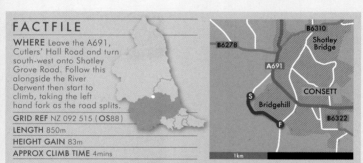

FACTFILE

WHERE Leave the A691, Cutlers' Hall Road and turn south-west onto Shotley Grove Road. Follow this alongside the River Derwent then start to climb, taking the left hand fork as the road splits.

GRID REF NZ 092 515 (**OS**88)

LENGTH 850m

HEIGHT GAIN 83m

APPROX CLIMB TIME 4mins

RATINGS

The climbs are rated from **1/10** to **10/10** within the context of the book. The rating is an amalgamation of gradient, length, the likely hostility of the riding conditions, and the condition of the surface. All the climbs are tough, therefore **1/10** equals 'hard', and **10/10** equals 'it's all you can do to keep your bike moving'. Some will suit you more than others; the saying 'horses for courses' applies, but all the **10/10** climbs will test any rider.

MAP KEY

Motorway	M1
A Road	A123
B Road	B1234
Minor Road	
Rail line	STATION
Hill route	S START ————— F FINISH
Town	TOWN
Scale	2km

TEESSIDE

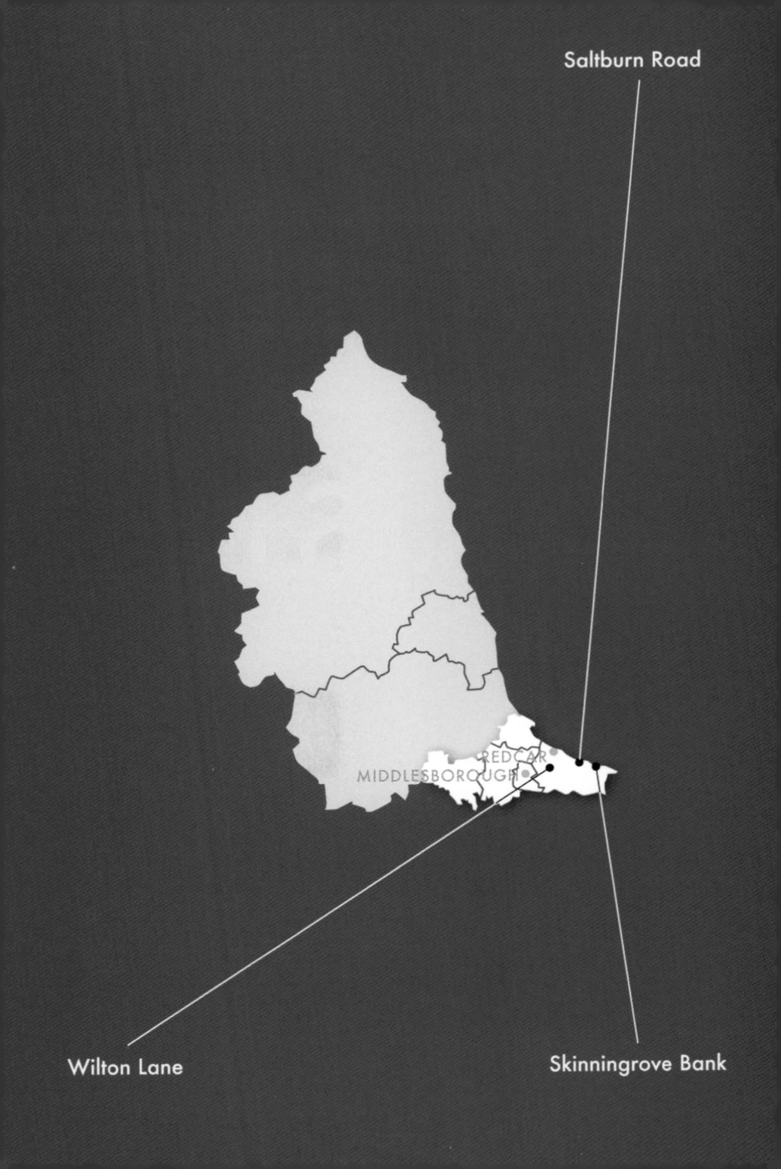

Saltburn Road

Wilton Lane

Skinningrove Bank

REDCAR
MIDDLESBOROUGH

RATING
1/10

SALTBURN ROAD

SALTBURN

The prospect of a hairpin bend can drag me to any corner of Britain. No matter how insignificant, a steep switchback will momentarily transport me to the grand mountain passes of the Alps or the Pyrenees. This climb may be only 300 metres long, but it's worth seeking out for a brief flirtation with some exotic corners and the sense that you could be riding the slopes of Alpe d'Huez. Head away from the seafront, bending left past the restaurant, to rise up to the first corner. At first the gradient is reasonably tame, but after the first bend it ramps up to the advertised 1-in-4. On the approach to the second corner you'll be thankful for a slight plateau, because it gets steeper once you're up and around it, now on to the final tough ramp to the junction at the top. At just a minute long, this climb is little more than a sprint, and hopefully you'll have enough in your legs to keep the pressure on all the way.

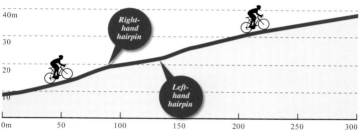

40m

30

20

10

0m   50   100   150   200   250   300

Right-hand hairpin

Left-hand hairpin

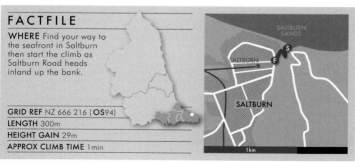

FACTFILE

WHERE Find your way to the seafront in Saltburn then start the climb as Saltburn Road heads inland up the bank.

GRID REF NZ 666 216 (OS94)

LENGTH 300m

HEIGHT GAIN 29m

APPROX CLIMB TIME 1min

SALTBURN SANDS

SALTBURN

SALTBURN

1km

RATING
5/10

SKINNINGROVE BANK

SKINNINGROVE

It was a wild day when I rode this climb, as you can see from the photograph opposite, with the North Sea in fine form, smashing its waves upon the battered shoreline. As the wind pounded my face on the way out of Skinningrove, I fought to the base of the climb, which rapidly veers up the cliffside and away from the water. Sweeping right, the slope is steep straight away, and it gets steeper – approaching 20% – as it picks its route upwards, bending left then right. A slight brow appears and then the twists become more pronounced between the high, grassy banks. The next brow comes as a great relief; here the slope eases back considerably, although not totally. You may think the hard work is behind you, but no, this climb has a nasty finish in store. Gradually increasing in pitch once again, the narrow road breaks left past a lone farmhouse into a short but vicious ramp, before eventually levelling at the T-junction.

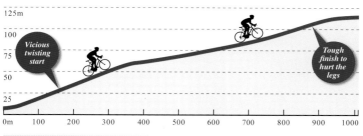

125m
100
75
50
25
0m   100   200   300   400   500   600   700   800   900   1000

Vicious twisting start

Tough finish to hurt the legs

FACTFILE

WHERE To the west of Loftus, head north from the A174 on Mill Lane into Skinningrove. Once in the village turn right onto Stone Row and then head to the seafront to start the climb.

GRID REF NZ 722 196 (OS94)

LENGTH 1050m

HEIGHT GAIN 108m

APPROX CLIMB TIME 5.5mins

RATING
5/10

WILTON LANE

WILTON

I was drawn to this climb the moment I saw the double chevrons on the OS map – these are a badge of honour all climbs wish they could wear, but only the special few are awarded. Whereas one chevron signifies a gradient between 14% and 20%, the double arrow marks a slope that exceeds 20%, so I was keen to see if this one lived up to its billing. Begin on the straight approach to the village; as the road bends slightly, you start to climb. You have to negotiate some traffic calming through the village, as well as a 90-degree bend, but otherwise the road is drama-free. This all changes as you bend left and ramp up into the woods. The narrow road writhes between the high banks and reaches its 20% gradient under the gloom of the branches overhead. Keep fighting the slope and keep searching for the light, as when the trees fade, so does the climb. It rounds a final corner to peak between some buildings.

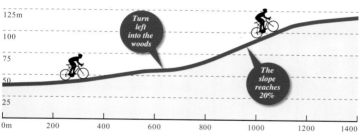

Turn left into the woods

The slope reaches 20%

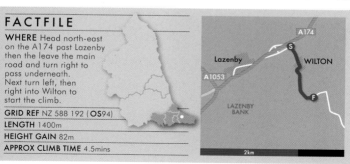

FACTFILE

WHERE Head north-east on the A174 past Lazenby then the leave the main road and turn right to pass underneath. Next turn left, then right into Wilton to start the climb.

GRID REF NZ 588 192 (OS94)

LENGTH 1400m

HEIGHT GAIN 82m

APPROX CLIMB TIME 4.5mins

COUNTY
DURHAM

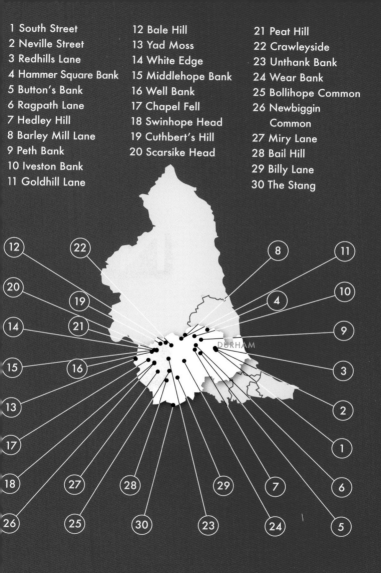

1 South Street
2 Neville Street
3 Redhills Lane
4 Hammer Square Bank
5 Button's Bank
6 Ragpath Lane
7 Hedley Hill
8 Barley Mill Lane
9 Peth Bank
10 Iveston Bank
11 Goldhill Lane
12 Bale Hill
13 Yad Moss
14 White Edge
15 Middlehope Bank
16 Well Bank
17 Chapel Fell
18 Swinhope Head
19 Cuthbert's Hill
20 Scarsike Head
21 Peat Hill
22 Crawleyside
23 Unthank Bank
24 Wear Bank
25 Bollihope Common
26 Newbiggin Common
27 Miry Lane
28 Bail Hill
29 Billy Lane
30 The Stang

DURHAM

RATING
3/10

SOUTH STREET

DURHAM

DISCLAIMER: to ride this climb you will have to disobey the road signs. It is a one-way street – I repeat, a one-way street – which, technically, you should not ride up. This, however, hasn't stopped it gaining fame as the centrepiece for the annual closed road, city centre races that commandeer its neatly arranged yet suitably rugged cobbles to pummel the legs of the competitors. If you're able to ride the event, then you will hit the base at speed, with the transition from smooth tarmac to abrasive pavé hitting like a hammer blow. As the road kicks up, twisting slightly right then immediately left, the narrow street is set on a 12% gradient, which is accentuated by the houses whose doors line its course. Very soon the hardest work is behind you, and although still juddering the wheels, the slope gradually begins to fade until the cobbles end, the road levels, and the smooth tarmac returns.

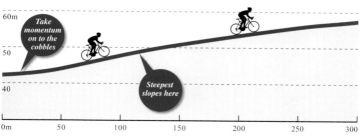

Take momentum on to the cobbles

Steepest slopes here

FACTFILE

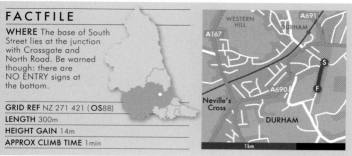

WHERE The base of South Street lies at the junction with Crossgate and North Road. Be warned though: there are NO ENTRY signs at the bottom.

GRID REF NZ 271 421 (OS88)	
LENGTH 300m	
HEIGHT GAIN 14m	
APPROX CLIMB TIME 1min	

RATING
1/10

NEVILLE STREET

DURHAM

In my quest to find South Street (see page 24) I discovered that Durham has many cobbled ascents, and as we all love riding them, I felt I could include more than one in the book. This is a pure power climb that requires one big effort to conquer both the uneven cobbles and unrelenting gradient in your quest for the summit at the T-junction. Right away you will notice that there is little order to the jumble of stones under your wheels. It reminds me of those found on the famous Koppenberg in Belgium, but this climb isn't quite as long or steep. The base lies on North Road; head downhill from the north end and take as much momentum as you can into the climb. Hold that speed to stay on top of your gear for as long as possible. At just 130 metres in length and gaining only 17 metres in altitude, Neville Street is one of the shortest hills I've documented, but it's certainly worth searching out.

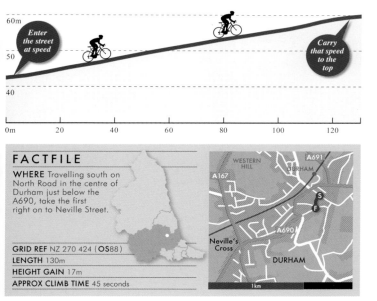

FACTFILE

WHERE Travelling south on North Road in the centre of Durham just below the A690, take the first right on to Neville Street.

GRID REF NZ 270 424 (OS88)	
LENGTH 130m	
HEIGHT GAIN 17m	
APPROX CLIMB TIME 45 seconds	

REDHILLS LANE

DURHAM

The whole of Durham is built on a hill with hardly an inch of flat ground, so if a climb is to stand out it has to be a little bit special: presenting Redhills Lane. Starting from the junction of Flass Street and Sutton Street, you gradually climb to the base, where the road narrows dramatically then heads off to the left. It's a two-way street but only really wide enough for a single car, so take care as you arc gently round to the right. The slope isn't too sharp lower down, but once out of this tight passage via a couple of even tighter pinch points, the road opens up. Ahead you see why you're here. Visibly ramping skywards and approaching 20%, the last 100-metre stretch is a killer. Short, yes. Sweet, no. It will punish the legs, but the end is in sight, so grin and bear it. When you reach the 90-degree corner at the top, push round all the way to the finish at the T-junction.

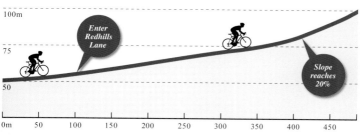

Enter Redhills Lane

Slope reaches 20%

FACTFILE

WHERE Start on Flass Street, heading south-west from the junction with Waddington Street and Sutton Street. Then continue on Redhills Lane as the road kinks left.

GRID REF NZ 264 425 (OS88)

LENGTH 485m

HEIGHT GAIN 50m

APPROX CLIMB TIME 2.5mins

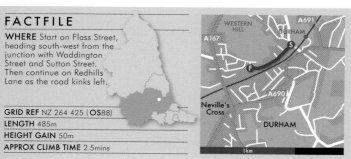

RATING
4/10

HAMMER SQUARE BANK

BEAMISH

After crossing Urpeth Burn at the base of the valley, this relatively short yet testing climb takes you up to the entrance to the Beamish Museum, which was built to provide a snapshot of the North-East's early twentieth-century industrial heritage. Back to the present, however, and to this climb, which, as you will discover, is almost entirely enveloped by foliage, aside from the first handful of metres. Under the intertwined branches of the trees above, the gradient varies little from a relentless 15%, and due to its permanent shade and abundance of flora, the surface is likely to be slippy year round. Thankfully, the slope never creeps that far above 15%; any higher and you'd have to deal with some wheel spin. Approaching the top a few glimmers of light break through the canopy, and the consistency of the slope falters to finish at the T-junction where you turn right for the museum.

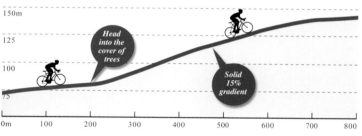

150m

125

100

75

0m   100   200   300   400   500   600   700   800

Head into the cover of trees

Solid 15% gradient

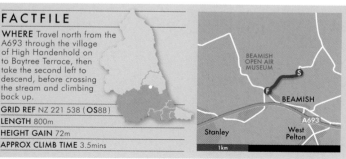

FACTFILE

WHERE Travel north from the A693 through the village of High Handenhold on to Baytree Terrace, then take the second left to descend, before crossing the stream and climbing back up.

GRID REF NZ 221 538 (OS88)

LENGTH 800m

HEIGHT GAIN 72m

APPROX CLIMB TIME 3.5mins

BEAMISH OPEN AIR MUSEUM

BEAMISH

A693

Stanley

West Pelton

1km

BUTTON'S BANK

WATERHOUSES

Button's Bank, or Wolsingham Road, is a kilometre of 10% gradient that rises out of Waterhouses, through West Wood, to the top of the ridge. There is little to see as you climb through the woodland in your search for the open sky at the top, so nothing to distract you from climbing. To begin, drop down out of Waterhouses and cross the narrow bridge. The road immediately plunges into the darkness beneath the trees. With little change in pitch or deviation in direction, there is not much to report on the lower slopes, but at roughly halfway the status quo is broken. Still deep in the wood, there's a brief levelling as the road twists first right then soon after left to resume its arduous 10% grind. Here the going is slightly tougher. You rise to a small clearing, then continue bending right under slightly less tree cover until you eventually hit the summit and at last catch sight of a view.

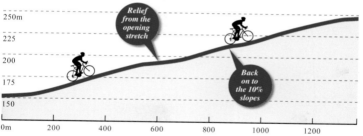

Relief from the opening stretch

Back on to the 10% slopes

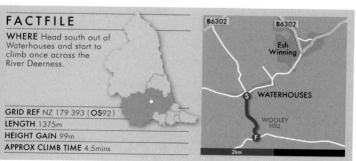

FACTFILE

WHERE Head south out of Waterhouses and start to climb once across the River Deerness.

GRID REF	NZ 179 393 (**OS**92)
LENGTH	1375m
HEIGHT GAIN	99m
APPROX CLIMB TIME	4.5mins

RAGPATH LANE

CORNSAY

One of a handful of vicious little roads in the hills to the south of Lanchester, Ragpath Lane is very popular with the locals, and although it takes a while to get going, when it does it will hit you for six. To find the true base, head east from the B6296 between Satley and Hollinside (towards Cornsay) and begin to climb once over the small moss-covered bridge. Heading left here you rise gently to a junction where you join another minor road and then head right. The slope continues very steadily for close to a kilometre. However, as the ridge begins to loom up ahead, it's clear the going is about to get tough, and the nerves will start to jangle. Pass a farm track on the right and bend slightly left; the gradient now kicks up and your gears will click down. Continue to bend gradually left as it gets steeper and steeper – up to 15% – before kinking right to finish abruptly beside a road joining from the right.

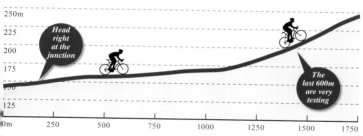

Head right at the junction

The last 600m are very testing

FACTFILE

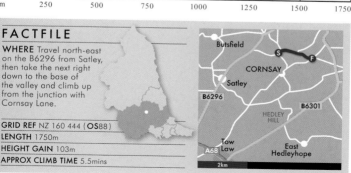

WHERE Travel north-east on the B6296 from Satley, then take the next right down to the base of the valley and climb up from the junction with Cornsay Lane.

GRID REF NZ 160 444 (**OS88**)

LENGTH 1750m

HEIGHT GAIN 103m

APPROX CLIMB TIME 5.5mins

RATING
4/10

HEDLEY HILL

EAST HEDLEYHOPE

I knew this climb held promise when I saw its snaking profile winding across the tight contours on the map. It didn't disappoint. As you approach the climb, by plunging down the opposite hillside, your eyes will scan the seemingly impenetrable wall ahead, looking for a way up and back out of the valley. At first there seems to be no escape; then, as you bend left, your exit up through the woods ahead is revealed. After a crossing over a small stream, the slope kicks up hard to a 20% left-hand corner, then backs off slightly to turn gently right up to a couple of houses. It becomes harder as you rise between the buildings; resume your right-hand trajectory and enjoy views out over the scrubland below, before heading for the finale in the woods. Bending left, the slope is a degree or so gentler, and you can build some speed as you snake towards the trees ahead for the final push to the summit.

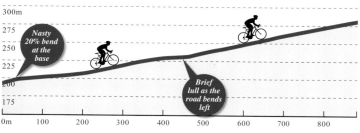

Nasty 20% bend at the base

Brief lull as the road bends left

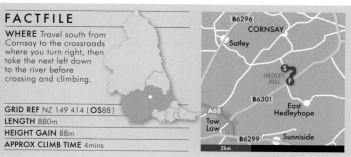

FACTFILE

WHERE Travel south from Cornsay to the crossroads where you turn right, then take the next left down to the river before crossing and climbing.

GRID REF NZ 149 414 (OS88)

LENGTH 880m

HEIGHT GAIN 88m

APPROX CLIMB TIME 4mins

BARLEY MILL LANE

CONSETT

There are many steep roads in and around Consett, but if you're looking for something hidden and pretty much traffic-free, then head here. Begin by leaving the busy A691 to ride south-west alongside the River Derwent. With the steep bank on your left, continue on the flat until you reach a fork where, passing the sign warning of the 15% gradient, you head left. Ramping immediately upwards, the rough, narrow road starts to bend left up the valley wall; skirting the fringes of the town, it's dotted with houses on the left and boasts grand views out to the right. The gradient is continually arduous, and I'd say the 15% advertised is a slight underestimation as you head into the trees. The surface will be slippery under your wheels on this last demanding push into the housing estate, where the slope thankfully eases for the gentle ride to the junction at the summit.

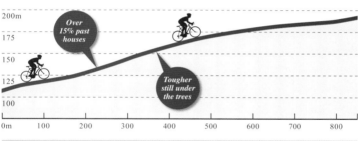

FACTFILE

WHERE Leave the A691, Cutlers' Hall Road, and turn south-west on to Shotley Grove Road. Follow this alongside the River Derwent then start to climb, taking the left hand fork as the road splits.

GRID REF NZ 092 515 (**OS**88)

LENGTH 850m

HEIGHT GAIN 83m

APPROX CLIMB TIME 4mins

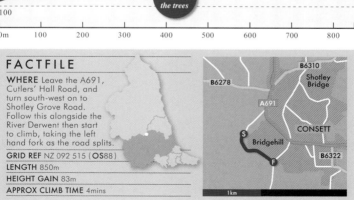

RATING
4/10

PETH BANK

LANCHESTER

Leave the centre of Lanchester and head east up the ridge. The climb starts as soon as you exit the main road, where large, sunken iron grilles line the gutter. After you pass a gradient sign, the road ramps up, bending left then right through some wickedly hard 20% bends, then left again to finish this – the hardest stretch – at a fake summit. Continue climbing gently, rising left to another brow followed by a short dip. Resist the urge to rest here; instead, click up a gear to build some momentum for the next section of climbing. Gaining an extra few kph before you hit the following testing set of bends pays rich dividends, as the gradient bites. As you round the long, sweeping right-hander, the radio mast at the top will come into view. This marks the summit, but it is still some way off; exit this section of bends and pedal through one final stretch of gentle climbing up to the finish at the T-junction.

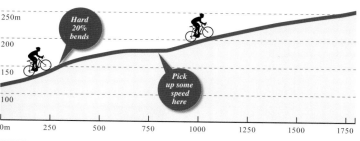

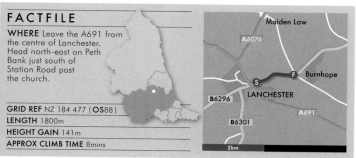

FACTFILE

WHERE Leave the A691 from the centre of Lanchester. Head north-east on Peth Bank just south of Station Road past the church.

GRID REF NZ 184 477 (OS88)

LENGTH 1800m

HEIGHT GAIN 141m

APPROX CLIMB TIME 8mins

IVESTON BANK

IVESTON

Start the ascent at the bottom of the gully on Stonyheap Lane. Head south-west, bending slightly left then right, to climb up to the junction with Lund's Lane. Here you fork right to join a narrow road nestled between high hedgerows. On the approach to the ridge ahead you enter a slight covering of trees and pass a set of warning signs that all hill climbers desire: the top warns of a 15% gradient, and the bottom of zig-zag bends. As you enter Iveston, the advertised slope twists between the houses on its way to a couple of more pronounced corners. First it heads left, but the steep road then kinks right to arrive at another left-hand turn, where 15% soon turns to 20% (if not a touch steeper). Pull yourself round this brilliant corner, then bend right on the still tough but gradually fading slope into the heart of the village to finish where the road levels.

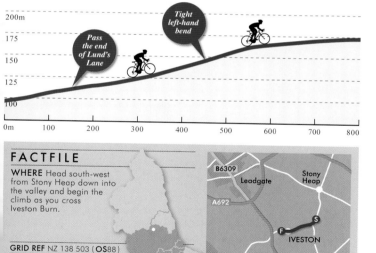

FACTFILE

WHERE Head south-west from Stony Heap down into the valley and begin the climb as you cross Iveston Burn.

GRID REF NZ 138 503 (OS88)

LENGTH 800m

HEIGHT GAIN 75m

APPROX CLIMB TIME 4mins

GOLDHILL LANE

CASTLESIDE

On a damp autumn morning, crawling up the wet tarmac of Goodhill Lane into the thick woods ahead is a pretty gloomy affair. Start from the T-junction at the bottom of the lane, following the sign to Waskerley; drop down to a small bridge, then rise up into the trees. Initially sharp, the gradient relents before increasing once more as the road bends right. It approaches 15% on its winding course towards a small clearing. From here the canopy above is replaced by rows of smaller trees either side; the tough climbing ends and the now shallower slope continues to meander upwards. The gradient ebbs and flows on this next section, enough to upset your rhythm and force multiple gear changes all the way up to a farm, where the character of the climb changes. Past the houses and across a cattle grid, you are suddenly on open, featureless ground for the remaining gentle climb to the summit.

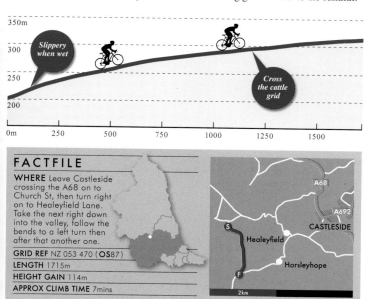

FACTFILE

WHERE Leave Castleside crossing the A68 on to Church St, then turn right on to Healeyfield Lane. Take the next right down into the valley, follow the bends to a left turn then after that another one.

GRID REF NZ 053 470 (OS87)	
LENGTH 1715m	
HEIGHT GAIN 114m	
APPROX CLIMB TIME 7mins	

RATING

6/10

BALE HILL

BLANCHLAND

A tale of three acts, Bale Hill will beat you up, allow you to recover, and then at the end come in for the kill. Begin by sweeping south out of Baybridge, crossing the border into County Durham and then the river, before heading up into the woods. The initially very tough ramp heads dead straight through an avenue of high banks and tall conifers, but it soon relents to meander through scattered clumps of trees and the odd building. Past the last house and up to a brow give it some welly, as after this you have a slight descent followed by a prolonged plateau on the approach to the final section of meadow. You climb to a brow across open ground lined with snow poles before dropping once more to catch sight of the rest of the climb. After a short roll across the vast emptiness you reach a killer 20% right-hand corner, which marks the beginning of the seemingly endless slog to the eventual summit.

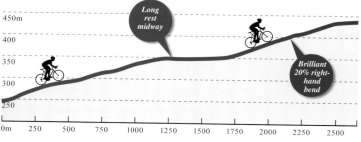

Long rest midway

Brilliant 20% right-hand bend

FACTFILE

WHERE Head west out of Blanchland then turn south in Baybridge and climb up out of the valley.

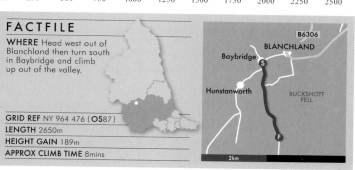

GRID REF NY 964 476 (**OS**87)

LENGTH 2650m

HEIGHT GAIN 189m

APPROX CLIMB TIME 8mins

RATING
4/10

YAD MOSS

FOREST-IN-TEESDALE

Although not quite Sir Ranulph Fiennes territory, it certainly feels like an adventure climbing up to and crossing the barren Yad Moss. Ride out from Middleton-in-Teesdale, roll up and down for a while, and then start the climb proper at the Forest-in-Teesdale sign. I haven't chosen many climbs that you can start in the big ring, but this is one. The gradient is very gentle at first so pick up speed and keep the large gear spinning for as long as you can. At the point where the road ramps up away from the last of the trees and past a couple of houses, I had to give in and change down, but when the course bent right and eased I engaged it once more. Next there's a fairly long stretch across a plateau before you dip through some snaking bends to the Langdon Beck Hotel and into the toughest part of the climb. A sharp rise bends left, but once through that you can settle down for the long, exposed quest to the summit.

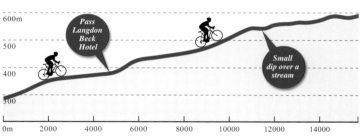

Pass Langdon Beck Hotel

Small dip over a stream

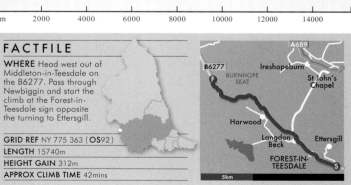

FACTFILE

WHERE Head west out of Middleton-in-Teesdale on the B6277. Pass through Newbiggin and start the climb at the Forest-in-Teesdale sign opposite the turning to Ettersgill.

GRID REF NY 775 363 (OS92)
LENGTH 15740m
HEIGHT GAIN 312m
APPROX CLIMB TIME 42mins

RATING
6/10

WHITE EDGE

WESTGATE

I pulled something in my back while riding this climb and had to limp up the second half in considerable discomfort. I can't attribute all the blame to the ascent, just most of it. As you rapidly approach the base down the even steeper Middlehope Bank, you can see White Edge in all its glory cutting an imposing and graphic swathe across the barren hillside. There is no disguising the fact that it will take some effort to conquer, so prepare yourself to do battle. Split into two sections, the first short stretch up to the 90-degree bend is slightly easier, but once round – and with no momentum left from the preceding drop – it's a grind all the way to the summit. Here you travel in an almost dead straight line on a consistently punishing slope framed by rough grass verges and crumbling stone walls. The torment goes on and on until you pass the top of Peat Hill and arrive at the top at the base of Scarsike Head.

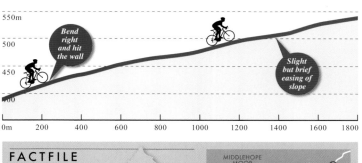

Bend right and hit the wall

Slight but brief easing of slope

FACTFILE

WHERE Climb out of Ireshopeburn up Well Bank, drop down Middlehope Bank to Middlehope Burn then climb back up to Scarsike Head.

GRID REF NY 911 414 (**OS**87)

LENGTH 1800m

HEIGHT GAIN 148m

APPROX CLIMB TIME 8.5mins

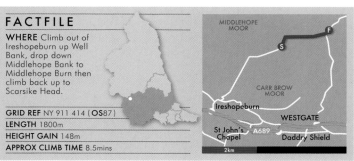

MIDDLEHOPE MOOR

F

S

CARR BROW MOOR

Ireshopeburn

WESTGATE

St John's Chapel

A689

Daddry Shield

2km

MIDDLEHOPE BANK

IRESHOPEBURN

There's no easy way to reach this short yet brutal climb; it lies in a quiet valley, protected on all sides by even stiffer climbs. In fact, in the space of a few square kilometres, you'll find arguably the highest concentration of killer hills anywhere in England. Depending on which route you choose to take here, one thing is likely: first, you will descend White Edge to reach the valley at the base, and hit the base at speed. Conserve as much momentum from the descent as you can and take that on to the rapidly increasing gradient in front of you. As you click down the gears, it just gets harder and harder until the slope reaches 20% and you approach a standstill. After the second of two slight brows, a small wood appears on the horizon; this marks the finish, encouraging you to dig that bit deeper as the road gently weaves left and right over the final few hundred metres.

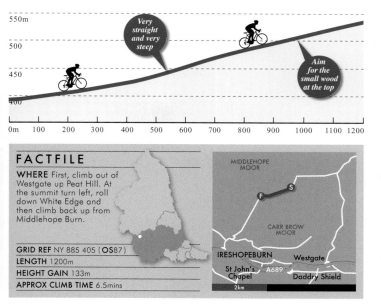

FACTFILE

WHERE First, climb out of Westgate up Peat Hill. At the summit turn left, roll down White Edge and then climb back up from Middlehope Burn.

GRID REF NY 885 405 (OS87)	
LENGTH 1200m	
HEIGHT GAIN 133m	
APPROX CLIMB TIME 6.5mins	

RATING
8/10

WELL BANK

IRESHOPEBURN

Mirroring its close neighbour and partner in pain Peat Hill (see page 64) just a couple of kilometres to the east, Well Bank concentrates its vicious climbing on its curvaceous lower slopes. Leave the A689 in Ireshopeburn; there's a short lull along the valley floor and over the River Wear before the road kinks slightly right and then up the daunting hillside. The slope approaches 20% almost immediately, forcing you to engage all your thrusters in your bid to escape the gravitational pull of Weardale. The series of savage bends between the various farmhouses will burn your fuel at an alarming rate and leave your tank all but empty as you round the last gruelling corner. Bending right past the lone house you're soon free of the harsh gradients. You can now float upwards through the tranquillity of vast open moorlands to reach the summit just before the road bends right.

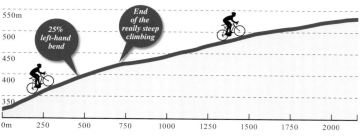

25% left-hand bend

End of the really steep climbing

FACTFILE

WHERE Head north from the A689 in Ireshopeburn, cross the River Wear, and then start to climb once past the entrance to a farm.

GRID REF NY 884 404 (OS87)

LENGTH 2150m

HEIGHT GAIN 212m

APPROX CLIMB TIME 13mins

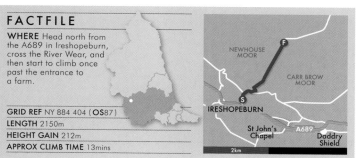

RATING
9/10

CHAPEL FELL

SAINT JOHN'S CHAPEL

Chapel Fell – the highest paved pass in England – comes complete with the tough gradient and frequently wild weather that befits its status. Pick your way out of Saint John's Chapel past a row of cottages to meet your first test: short and steep. This is followed by a drop from where you will see the road that lies ahead. Next, a very sharp dip is followed by an identically sharp rise, so any momentum through here will evaporate as quickly as it was created. Drag yourself from this hollow, easing up to a cattle grid: the start of your killer slog to the summit. Part-way along this decent surface is a fake brow where you're allowed a brief moment's rest while crossing a bridge. Over the stream is a leg-breaking wrench up, left then right. Cross the cattle grid to finish next to the old quarry. With nothing but grassland between you and the sky, you'll reach the summit windswept and aching.

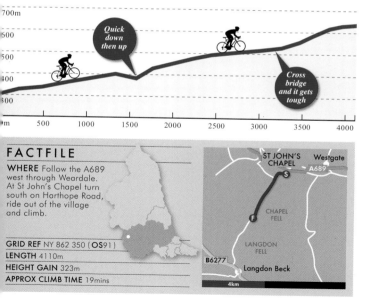

FACTFILE

WHERE Follow the A689 west through Weardale. At St John's Chapel turn south on Harthope Road, ride out of the village and climb.

GRID REF NY 862 350 (OS91)

LENGTH 4110m

HEIGHT GAIN 323m

APPROX CLIMB TIME 19mins

RATING 8/10

SWINHOPE HEAD

WESTGATE

Running parallel to the infamous Chapel Fell (see page 56) just a few kilometres to the west, the road up to Swinhope Head reaches almost the same altitude as its neighbour, but not quite. As you can see on the profile below, the climbing comes in two sections, and after the initial sharp ramp, the first stretch is the easiest. Pick your way between the stone walls and isolated cottages; you soon find yourself on exposed moorland where the gradient subsides before you begin to descend. The second stretch of climbing is tough from the moment you leave the gully. Once past another group of cottages you have to negotiate a gate to enter Westerhope Moor. Here the road sweeps round giant corners across barren hillside before ending on a nasty finish: a short stretch of leg-breaking 15% gradient that rises between the snow poles to reveal stupendous views on the other side.

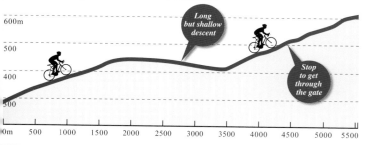

FACTFILE

WHERE Travelling east from St John's Chapel leave the A689 and continue on Pleasant Row. Then take the right turn following the signs to Newbiggin.

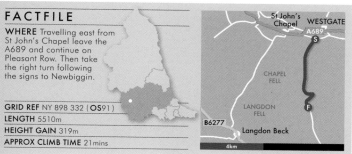

GRID REF NY 898 332 (OS91)	
LENGTH 5510m	
HEIGHT GAIN 319m	
APPROX CLIMB TIME 21mins	

CUTHBERT'S HILL

ROOKHOPE

Cuthbert's Hill sits in the far north of the vast Pennines, and is virtually the only sign of human presence on this empty moor, leading you away from the wilderness and down into Blanchland. Begin the ascent just under half a mile west of the village of Rookhope at a T-junction and head towards Blanchland. After a short rise then a short dip, you cross a bridge, and then you're on to a 20% gradient that leads to a beautiful, sweeping right-hand bend. After this you can sit back down for a while, but it's far from easy. Up ahead the road bends round to the left, eases some more, and then the snow poles start. You next find yourself on a fantastic barren plateau surrounded by nothing but the chattering grouse. Take some time to soak in the awesome emptiness. Follow the road up to a left-hand rise, then a right-hand dip, then up again round to the left. Finish as you cross a cattle grid.

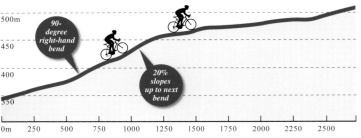

90-degree right-hand bend

20% slopes up to next bend

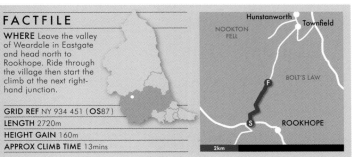

FACTFILE

WHERE Leave the valley of Weardale in Eastgate and head north to Rookhope. Ride through the village then start the climb at the next right-hand junction.

GRID REF NY 934 451 (OS87)

LENGTH 2720m

HEIGHT GAIN 160m

APPROX CLIMB TIME 13mins

SCARSIKE HEAD

ROOKHOPE

There had been a reasonable snowfall in the few days before I rode this climb. Although the roads were clear, there was still a good covering on the hillsides, which made them look even more rugged and remote than they already are. Start the ascent just west of Rookhope, where you head south out of the valley and over the stone bridge crossing Rookhope Burn. The road bends immediately left, climbs hard up to a right-hand hairpin, then continues to rise steeply for a while before easing back and almost levelling on the approach to a small group of trees. As you reach the trees, the road switches left then right, and it's a tough 15% through the tight bends that mark the mid-point of the ascent. From here the sense of isolation is wonderful, and even better under dark grey skies, as you approach the finale: a nasty, prolonged 15% ramp that drags you to the summit just shy of the turning to Westgate.

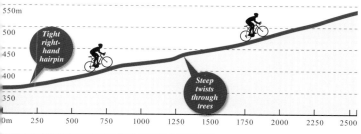

Tight right-hand hairpin

Steep twists through trees

FACTFILE

WHERE Travel west from Rookhope then take the first left across the river and head south over Lintzgarth Common.

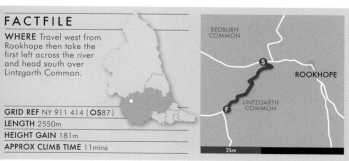

REDBURN COMMON

ROOKHOPE

LINTZGARTH COMMON

2km

GRID REF NY 911 414 (OS87)

LENGTH 2550m

HEIGHT GAIN 181m

APPROX CLIMB TIME 11mins

RATING

8/10

PEAT HILL

WESTGATE

Of the two routes out of Weardale up on to Middlehope Moor, Peat Hill out of Westgate just sneaks it as the toughest route. Leave the A689 in the centre of the village and, after rounding the first couple of houses, take a good look at the task ahead of you. Snaking its way through the buildings ahead is a seriously steep road. From this first glimpse you'll know it's going to be a killer, but this isn't even the toughest part. Make your way out of the village and – already at maximum effort – hit three achingly steep corners, first left, then right, then left again. Get through these ruthless bends – the last of which is incredibly rough – and you'll almost be through the worst, but there's still one more wicked stretch before the gradient relents. All that's left now is for you to follow the crooked undulating path to the summit and finish at the junction where the road heads down in both directions.

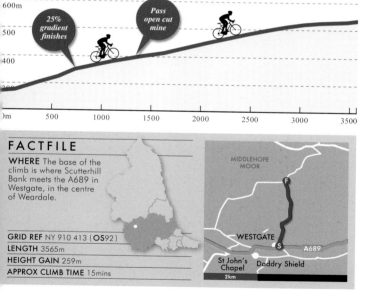

FACTFILE

WHERE The base of the climb is where Scutterhill Bank meets the A689 in Westgate, in the centre of Weardale.

GRID REF NY 910 413 (OS92)
LENGTH 3565m
HEIGHT GAIN 259m
APPROX CLIMB TIME 15mins

RATING 7/10

CRAWLEYSIDE

STANHOPE

The village of Stanhope lies in Weardale, with stiff climbs leaving town from either side. The best option, heading north, is the ascent through Crawleyside. You climb steeply from the off and climb gradually steeper until you reach a sweeping right-hand bend. Once past the Crawleyside sign, grind your way up the punishing 20% slopes through the town. The end of the opening section is marked by a cattle grid and then you hit the open moor, which brings a change in gradient. The gentler gradient doesn't last long, and the road kicks up towards a farmhouse on the left. Pass this house, bend right, and enjoy a short breather as the road dips before the flat approach to the finale. The final effort to reach the top of the moor is an arrow-straight 14% section followed by a hard right-hand bend. Now all that stands between you and the summit is some very gentle climbing out of Weardale.

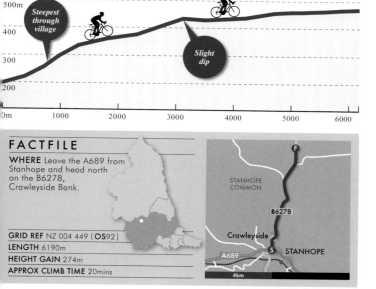

FACTFILE

WHERE Leave the A689 from Stanhope and head north on the B6278, Crawleyside Bank.

GRID REF NZ 004 449 (OS92)	
LENGTH 6190m	
HEIGHT GAIN 274m	
APPROX CLIMB TIME 20mins	

RATING
5/10

UNTHANK BANK

STANHOPE

'Wow! Look at those bends,' I laughed when I first saw this road. It didn't make the cut for *100 Greatest Cycling Climbs* because of its proximity to the more frequently travelled Crawleyside just opposite, but it was a hard decision to leave it out. Make your way out of Stanhope, avoiding the ford if the river is high, and begin the climb once over a small railway line. The first gentle rise leads you to a right-hand bend; then it's straight up 17% into the best set of tight, snaking bends this side of the Stelvio Pass. Some climbs are great because of their length, others because of the severity of their gradient. A few more – such as Unthank Bank – are outstanding because of the character they pack into just a few hundred metres of tarmac. Bank left, up, then sweep right and left. Before you know it, it's over. You haven't reached the top though, far from it – there's a lot more climbing to the summit, but this ride is all about those twisting bends.

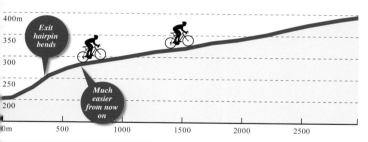

FACTFILE

WHERE Leave the A689 south on to the B6278 following the road right, then left across the river and left again back on itself. Then turn right, cross the rail lines and begin the climb.

GRID REF NY 984 365 (**OS**92)

LENGTH 2920m

HEIGHT GAIN 195m

APPROX CLIMB TIME 13mins

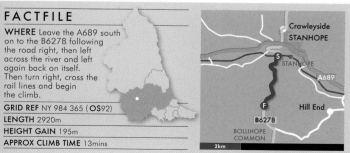

WEAR BANK

WOLSINGHAM

Rising from the wonderful steel bridge that spans the River Wear, this climb is the furthest east of the many that head south out of Weardale. Although not as harsh as its westerly neighbours, it's a serious challenge nonetheless. Once across the bridge, the road bends instantly right, then left; after that it starts to climb across a second bridge and out of sight. It isn't long before the twisting slope hits 15% and you start on the toughest part of the ascent, in the shadow of the trees above. Continually weaving gently right and left, you reach a slight brow; here the gradient eases for a while, before it kicks up again almost to the point where you change direction. Following a long left-hand corner, the road then bends abruptly left at the base of a dead-end track that continues straight on. Round this corner the slope relents, allowing you to gently pedal out the final few hundred metres to the top.

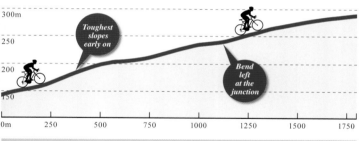

Toughest slopes early on

Bend left at the junction

FACTFILE

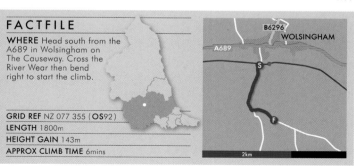

WHERE Head south from the A689 in Wolsingham on The Causeway. Cross the River Wear then bend right to start the climb.

GRID REF NZ 077 355 (OS92)

LENGTH 1800m

HEIGHT GAIN 143m

APPROX CLIMB TIME 6mins

RATING

7/10

BOLLIHOPE COMMON

STANHOPE

This is one of those roads that you wish would go on forever, such is its beauty. You start the ascent in the gullied landscape surrounding the Bollihope Burn – a tranquil idyll of neat grass verges and bubbling brooks hidden beneath high, mossy banks. The peace ends when you begin to climb, though. As the road rears up into a vicious 20% right-hand hairpin, you're dragged kicking and screaming into the heart of the common. Never as steep again, the climb is still a challenge, although not on the lower slopes; these are just a joy to ride. With nothing either side of you aside from rolling hills as far as the eye can see, you're free to ride gently to the first brow and enjoy 500 metres of flat before embarking on the finale. Twisting its way across the empty hillside, this section is a proper grind. Slight changes in direction pepper the stiff gradient that eventually leads to the summit at a small car park.

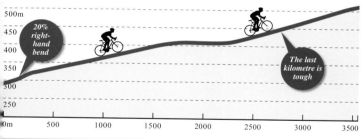

500m
450
400
350
300
250
0m   500   1000   1500   2000   2500   3000   3500

20% right-hand bend

The last kilometre is tough

FACTFILE

WHERE Head out of Stanhope on the B6278, up Unthank Bank, then past Catterick Moss before dropping down to start the climb once over Bollihope Burn.

GRID REF NY 992 318 (OS92)

LENGTH 3550m

HEIGHT GAIN 223m

APPROX CLIMB TIME 13mins

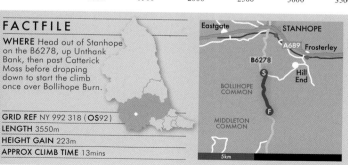

Eastgate   STANHOPE
                A689 Frosterley
            B6278
        S   Hill End
BOLLIHOPE
COMMON
            F
MIDDLETON
COMMON

5km

RATING
5/10

NEWBIGGIN COMMON

Once again I am breaking my own rule of not documenting both sides of the same ridge. Nevertheless, here's Newbiggin Common, the climb that shares its summit with Swinhope Head (see page 58) to the north. It is fractionally longer than its opposing neighbour and has a slightly stiffer average gradient at just under 6%. The start is abrupt, heading up the narrow road between sheep-filled roads towards Westgate. Continue north between the seemingly never-ending stone walls and through an increasingly bleak landscape until you reach a gate next to a white farmhouse. Pass through this and dip down to cross Flushiemere Beck and a couple of cattle grids, where the scenery becomes even more dramatic. The walls disappear and you embark on a long trek to a lonely summit. With no protection and in the wrong conditions the mild 6% slope can feel like 60% here (trust me), so check the forecast before you ride.

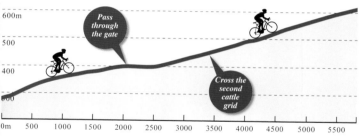

Pass through the gate

Cross the second cattle grid

600m
500
400
300
0m   500   1000   1500   2000   2500   3000   3500   4000   4500   5000   5500

FACTFILE

WHERE Leave the B6277 heading north into Newbiggin then turn left to head north out of the village.

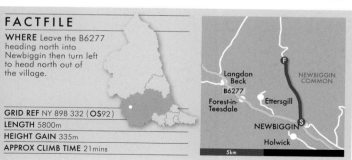

Langdon Beck
B6277
Forest-in-Teesdale
Ettersgill
NEWBIGGIN COMMON
NEWBIGGIN
Holwick
5km

GRID REF NY 898 332 (OS92)

LENGTH 5800m

HEIGHT GAIN 335m

APPROX CLIMB TIME 21mins

RATING
7/10

MIRY LANE

NEWBIGGIN

At just 800 metres long this climb doesn't really stand up to its close neighbours – it lacks the drama of crossing an exposed moor – but it is damned steep at least. As you leave the main road and head into Newbiggin, there's a gentle rise to the T-junction. This permits you to prepare for the onslaught ahead. After the right-hand turn the next 600 metres average over 13% (although in some spots it's much steeper). Head between the houses on the (almost) 20% slope up to a pronounced brow; it eases as you sweep left. Make the most of this corner and catch your breath, as once through it's eyeballs out to the top. Bending slightly right yet following a direct route up the bank, you heave your bike up towards a solitary farmhouse. Here, following a more pronounced kink, the road heads further right, and the slope finally fades on its approach to the finish at the junction.

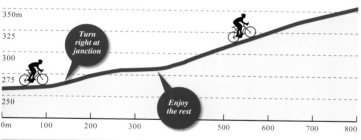

Turn right at junction

Enjoy the rest

FACTFILE

WHERE Begin the climb by leaving the B6277 in Newbiggin heading up to join Miry lane at the T-junction where you turn right to continue.

GRID REF NY 921 572 (OS92)	
LENGTH 800m	
HEIGHT GAIN 97m	
APPROX CLIMB TIME 5mins	

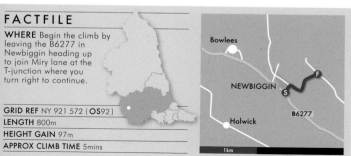

BAIL HILL

MICKLETON

You begin this climb by leaving Mickleton on a very slight gradient and negotiating three distinct 90-degree turns – left, right, then left again. There is no real altitude gain to speak of at this point. Exiting the third turn, things change – the slope now climbs rapidly towards a small clump of trees on the horizon. This straight and narrow stretch up to a right-hand kink will sting the legs. Round the next bend the steep stuff continues, up to a brow next to a farm. Once you reach this peak the slope is never as tough again, but there is still a fair way to go to the top. On an undulating path between the fields, with a couple of spikes in gradient and a wicked left-hand bend, you soon arrive at the final stretch. On the horizon you will see the radio transmitter that marks the summit. Get out of the saddle and chase it round the final right-hand bend to finish just shy of the junction with Botany Road and Fell Lane.

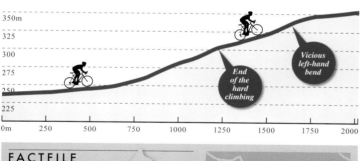

End of the hard climbing

Vicious left-hand bend

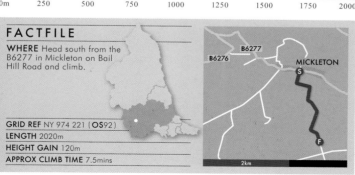

FACTFILE

WHERE Head south from the B6277 in Mickleton on Bail Hill Road and climb.

GRID REF NY 974 221 (OS92)

LENGTH 2020m

HEIGHT GAIN 120m

APPROX CLIMB TIME 7.5mins

BILLY LANE

MICKLETON

Bridging the gap between the B6279 and the B6282 to the east of Mickleton, Billy Lane climbs up to the edge of the wonderful Woodland Fell. Leave the B6279 and head north; you first drop sharply down and naturally build good speed to take into the bottom of the climb. You may hope this will get you up at least the first 100 metres before you have to pedal. Unfortunately, once you reach the base, there are 50 metres of flat that rob you of your precious momentum, ensuring you have to work right from the start. These lower slopes are hard, hitting 14% at their steepest. They quickly back off (quite considerably) but then kick up once more to where the road bends right and disappears over a brow. What follows is a small descent, and this time you can carry the momentum into the rest of the climb, which starts stiffly after the cattle grid before fading on the approach to the T-junction at the top.

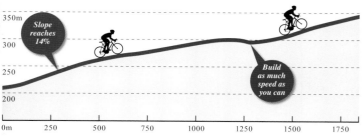

Slope reaches 14%

Build as much speed as you can

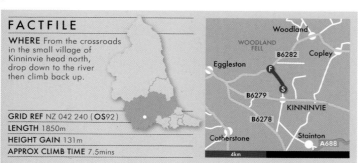

FACTFILE

WHERE From the crossroads in the small village of Kinninvie head north, drop down to the river then climb back up.

GRID REF NZ 042 240 (OS92)

LENGTH 1850m

HEIGHT GAIN 131m

APPROX CLIMB TIME 7.5mins

RATING 7/10

THE STANG

BARNARD CASTLE

I have documented the south face of the Stang in both *100 Greatest Cycling Climbs* and *Cycling Climbs of Yorkshire*, but the north face is almost its equal. It's longer than its partner and also gains slightly more elevation, but its average gradient of just 5% compared to 6.5% does make this climb a slightly easier challenge. The lower slopes are quite gentle; then over a brow there's a short 17% descent before a levelling where the real action begins. Once into the forest, the road comes to life. Surrounded by trees, the slope gets tougher and tougher. Unlike the southern side, which is totally exposed, the enveloping forest offers some protection from any wind, but its punishing slopes still batter the legs. The varying but consistently tough gradient comes to a peak through a series of tight bends that hit 20% at their apex, and which deliver you to the plateau and the summit at the border with Yorkshire.

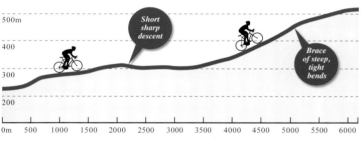

Short sharp descent

Brace of steep, tight bends

FACTFILE

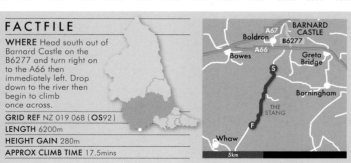

WHERE Head south out of Barnard Castle on the B6277 and turn right on to the A66 then immediately left. Drop down to the river then begin to climb once across.

GRID REF NZ 019 068 (**OS**92)

LENGTH 6200m

HEIGHT GAIN 280m

APPROX CLIMB TIME 17.5mins

NORTHUMBERLAND

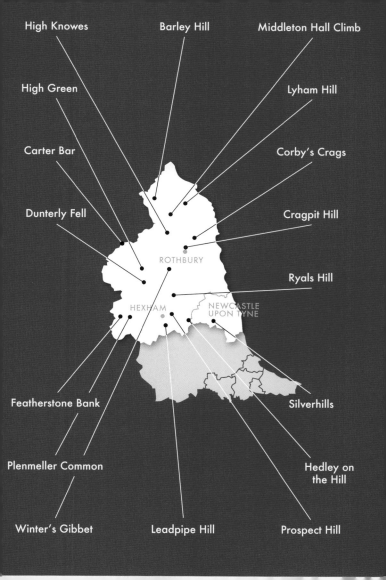

High Knowes

Barley Hill

Middleton Hall Climb

High Green

Lyham Hill

Carter Bar

Corby's Crags

Dunterly Fell

Cragpit Hill

ROTHBURY

Ryals Hill

HEXHAM

NEWCASTLE
UPON TYNE

Featherstone Bank

Silverhills

Plenmeller Common

Hedley on
the Hill

Winter's Gibbet

Leadpipe Hill

Prospect Hill

RATING

3/10

SILVERHILLS

GATESHEAD, TYNE AND WEAR

If you're a cyclist living in an urban conurbation, you'll be sure to crave a quick route out of town and (more importantly) somewhere decent nearby to test your legs. For riders in the Gateshead area, Silverhills provides the perfect spot. There are two stiff climbs up this mound; the quieter, steeper, and hence better of the two is Banesley Lane. To begin, leave the roundabout on the edge of town and enter the village of Lady Park; spin your legs and follow the road round to the left. A white line on the tarmac marks the start of the hill climb course, and the point at which the gradient starts to bite. Next there's a sharp ramp and a levelling. Following a gentle stretch, the going is hard again before you enter a smooth, wide S-bend. After this comes the hard push to the top. The extremely rough road bends round to the left leading to a brow, a dip, a plateau, and finally a small rise to the finish.

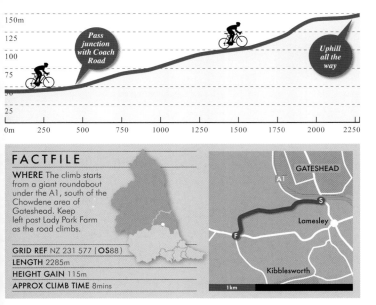

Pass junction with Coach Road

Uphill all the way

FACTFILE

WHERE The climb starts from a giant roundabout under the A1, south of the Chowdene area of Gateshead. Keep left past Lady Park Farm as the road climbs.

GRID REF NZ 231 577 (**OS**88)

LENGTH 2285m

HEIGHT GAIN 115m

APPROX CLIMB TIME 8mins

HEDLEY ON THE HILL

PAINSHAWFIELD

I had a look at two routes up to Hedley on the Hill, and this one – the MH11 hill climb course – excited me most. If you ride to the base via Stocksfield or through Painshawfield, you'll gain significant altitude before you turn south from New Ridley Road to begin the climb proper. Passing the 'unsuitable for HGVs' sign, you will spy the first of many changes in gradient. It's tough until you reach a zig-zag road sign where you can relax for a short while. Heading right, you quickly return to the steeper slopes and then, when the advertised corners finally arrive, things get really interesting. First you bend sharp left where the slope is even tougher, then you sweep right, then left, then hard right again. After a short straight, the testing gradient finally gives way and you round the final corner to line up for the summit, which arrives just before the sign for Hedley on the Hill.

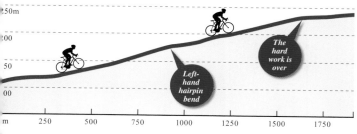

The hard work is over

Left-hand hairpin bend

FACTFILE

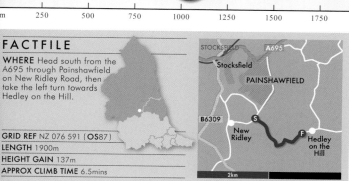

WHERE Head south from the A695 through Painshawfield on New Ridley Road, then take the left turn towards Hedley on the Hill.

GRID REF NZ 076 591 (OS87)

LENGTH 1900m

HEIGHT GAIN 137m

APPROX CLIMB TIME 6.5mins

LEADPIPE HILL

SLALEY

As you will see from the map below, this is a road to nowhere, one that finishes deep in the Slaley Forest. Although my cycling mind doesn't see it that way – instead of a dead end, it sees a 'summit finish!' Bearing south from the B6306, you encounter a few undulations before the road bottoms out and begins to rise very gently towards the ridge ahead. For a while all is calm; then, rounding a slight left-hand bend, you will see the road ramp skyward. Here, the tranquillity ends. For close to 500 metres it just gets harder and harder. Heading due south with no deviation, this punishing incline will have you spouting all sorts of colourful language as you crawl up to the pronounced and welcome brow. Once over the brow you can relax; sit back down and enjoy rolling through a landscape of thick evergreen forest towards the finish at the entrance to the Ladycross Quarry.

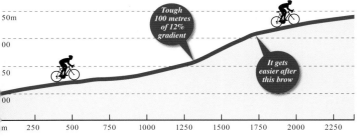

Tough 100 metres of 12% gradient

It gets easier after this brow

FACTFILE

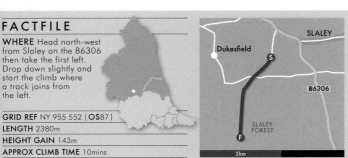

WHERE Head north-west from Slaley on the B6306 then take the first left. Drop down slightly and start the climb where a track joins from the left.

GRID REF NY 955 552 (OS87)

LENGTH 2380m

HEIGHT GAIN 143m

APPROX CLIMB TIME 10mins

RATING 7/10

PROSPECT HILL

CORBRIDGE

This is my new favourite Northumbrian climb. As soon as I saw its zig-zag course on the map, I knew it would be brilliant. And I wasn't disappointed – it's an absolute classic. Not quite tight enough to be labeled hairpins, the climb's six distinct 90-degree bends break up the length of the course at exact intervals from bottom to top, book-ending some seriously taxing straights. You're permitted a comfortable start up to the first corner, and then the hard work begins. The straights vary between a tough 10 and 15%, but the regularity of the bends ensures you continually have a point ahead to aim for. Rounding each corner you can put the struggle of the previous stretch behind you and start mentally fresh up the next – think of it as an intense interval training session (but a lot more fun). From both a rider's and spectator's point of view, this is the perfect course for a hill climb race – knock yourself out.

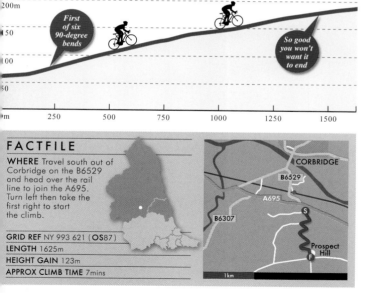

FACTFILE

WHERE Travel south out of Corbridge on the B6529 and head over the rail line to join the A695. Turn left then take the first right to start the climb.

GRID REF NY 993 621 (OS87)

LENGTH 1625m

HEIGHT GAIN 123m

APPROX CLIMB TIME 7mins

FEATHERSTONE BANK

HALTWHISTLE

[T]he jungle of lanes to the south-west of Haltwhistle hides a wealth of tiny climbs, [a]nd no matter how insignificant, the authorities seem to have assigned them all a [st]eep gradient sign. From 14% through to 20%, there is hardly a road left unadorned. [St]anding out from the crowd is this climb: Featherstone Bank. Short but perfectly [fo]rmed, the ascent starts to rise gently as you leave the banks of the River South [T]yne. Past the entrance to Featherstone Castle, the first left-hand corner bends 90 [d]egrees. Here you will be forced from your saddle as you start a short straight up to [th]e next deviation, this time heading right. The gradient is a uniform 12% as the road [c]uts across the bank to the woods at the top and heads towards the testing finale. [B]ending left under the trees, the slope momentarily reaches 20% before subsiding [o]ver the brow and petering out a few metres later.

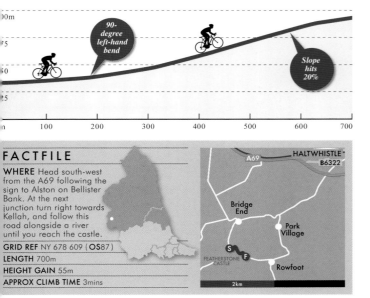

FACTFILE

WHERE Head south-west from the A69 following the sign to Alston on Bellister Bank. At the next junction turn right towards Kellah, and follow this road alongside a river until you reach the castle.

GRID REF NY 678 609 (OS87)

LENGTH 700m

HEIGHT GAIN 55m

APPROX CLIMB TIME 3mins

PLENMELLER COMMON

HALTWHISTLE

Heading south from Haltwhistle and crossing the solitude of Plenmeller Common, this is a rollercoaster of a climb, but one with far more up than down. Once through Plenmeller you begin to rise sharply between neat stone walls and into some woods ahead. Here the road kinks left, dips down, then rises in waves of steep then shallow gradient up to the next small clump of trees. After a slight plateau, there's a sharp plunge down to the left followed by an even sharper kick up, so take as much momentum as you can into this. The scenery now opens out to reveal empty moorland, with the road cutting its way over the hillside in front of you. It's a struggle up to the brow ahead, but once surmounted the rest of the ride is a breeze, levelling then dipping then climbing gently again. Wallow in the splendour of your surroundings as you tackle the remaining exposed slopes to where the climb finally tops out.

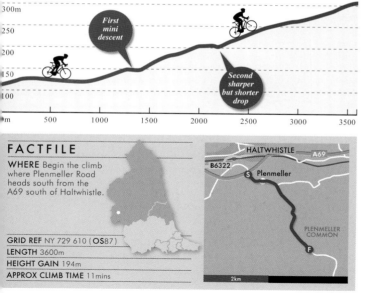

FACTFILE

WHERE Begin the climb where Plenmeller Road heads south from the A69 south of Haltwhistle.

GRID REF NY 729 610 (OS87)

LENGTH 3600m

HEIGHT GAIN 194m

APPROX CLIMB TIME 11mins

RYALS HILL

RYAL

Ryals Hill is the cornerstone of the annual Beaumont Trophy bike race, one of the monuments of the British bike-racing calendar and a climb that has forced many cyclists to their knees – for this it will always have a place in cycling folklore. A small stone bridge in a hollow marks the start. A short ascent is followed by a levelling at a crossroads, and then a dip down leads into another short, sharp rise. After this you climb steadily towards a farmhouse on the horizon. Over the lip you come face to face with the first of the twin perils that await: two 1-in-6 ramps that will stop you in your tracks. Grind your way up the dead straight road, passing the faded names of previous riders painted on the road, to crest the first brow. Then bang! You're hit with the hammer blow of having to do it all again. Thankfully, this second ramp is a fraction easier. Finish just past the white line painted on the road.

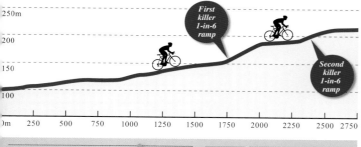

FACTFILE

WHERE Leave the A68 at the junction with the B6342 heading east, then immediately turn right on to the minor road. Follow this to a dip at Hallington Mill and start the climb from the bridge.

GRID REF NZ 007 742 (**OS87**)

LENGTH 2750m

HEIGHT GAIN 112m

APPROX CLIMB TIME 10mins

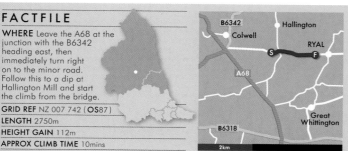

RATING
6/10

DUNTERLY FELL

Compact and bijou, this 1,400-metre ascent set on an 8% average gradient is a delight. At the base (on the junction) there's a slight hump, then an easing. Ahead you will see the climb draped across the fell. Cross a cattle grid; after this the pitch increases and it continues stiff up to a right-hand bend, where you drop a little before hitting a hard ramp into a small wood. Follow the road round to the left into some more strenuous climbing that leads to a slight easing – just long enough for a couple of resistance-free pedal revs before the climb ramps up once more. Ahead you will see the road bend right, where it becomes steeper still. Arcing out of sight, the end to this arduous corner refuses to reveal itself. Round and round you bend until, at the point where your legs are screaming 'No more!', you reach the brow. This marks the end of the hard work, but it's not the top – that lies a few hundred metres further on.

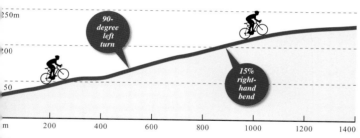

250m

200

50

m   200   400   600   800   1000   1200   1400

90-degree left turn

15% right-hand bend

FACTFILE

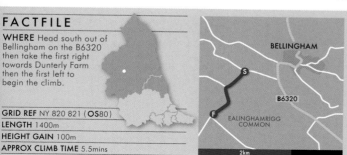

WHERE Head south out of Bellingham on the B6320 then take the first right towards Dunterly Farm then the first left to begin the climb.

BELLINGHAM

B6320

EALINGHAMRIGG COMMON

2km

GRID REF NY 820 821 (**OS**80)

LENGTH 1400m

HEIGHT GAIN 100m

APPROX CLIMB TIME 5.5mins

HIGH GREEN

BELLINGHAM

The wild, stunning climb that lies on the southern edge of the Kielder Forest will truly take you into the back of beyond. Before you get to the base (via the village of Greenhaugh) you have a few waves in the road to tackle. But following the last, rapid little drop and a rusting cattle grid you can begin your quest for the summit. It's hard right away. Trudge up past two small clumps of woodland, the second of which hides the grand Highgreen Manor. Continue on to a third small clump of trees; there follows a slight dip from where you will see the remainder of the climb disappearing across the desolate wilderness. At the junction, head right and follow the road as it arcs left past the turning to Sundaysight. Now you have just the finale to go, which unfortunately gets tougher and tougher before eventually fading away to reveal spectacular views over the eastern half of Northumberland.

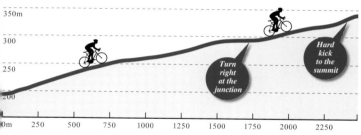

350m
300
250
200
0m   250   500   750   1000   1250   1500   1750   2000   2250

Turn right at the junction

Hard kick to the summit

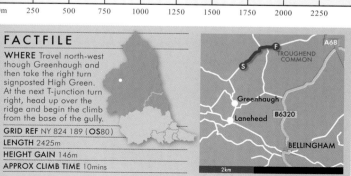

FACTFILE

WHERE Travel north-west though Greenhaugh and then take the right turn signposted High Green. At the next T-junction turn right, head up over the ridge and begin the climb from the base of the gully.

GRID REF NY 824 189 (OS80)

LENGTH 2425m

HEIGHT GAIN 146m

APPROX CLIMB TIME 10mins

A68
TROUGHEND COMMON
F
S
Greenhaugh
B6320
Lanehead
BELLINGHAM
2km

WINTER'S GIBBET

ELSDON

This climb takes its name from the gibbet at its peak, first erected in 1791 to display the body of famed criminal William Winter. The present gibbet was installed sometime later as a curiosity, complete with a fake head. Head south-east out of Elsdon to start the climb. Fiendishly, the sharpest stretch is right at the bottom, and is sure to make your legs burn with lactic acid, ensuring the rest of the climb is that much tougher. The smooth road soon eases, bending left then right. Continue climbing the steady gradient until you reach a steep left-hand bend that leads to a fake brow, followed by a short dip. The edge of the road begins to disintegrate here, so ride wide and try to build up some speed to carry you towards the top. Once up the next and final hard stretch and over the brow, you will spot the gibbet. The hard work is now behind you. Push on up the ever-decreasing slope to finish alongside Harwood Forest.

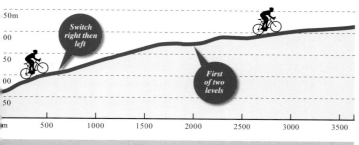

Switch right then left

First of two levels

| m | 500 | 1000 | 1500 | 2000 | 2500 | 3000 | 3500 |

FACTFILE

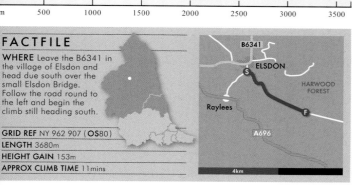

WHERE Leave the B6341 in the village of Elsdon and head due south over the small Elsdon Bridge. Follow the road round to the left and begin the climb still heading south.

GRID REF NY 962 907 (OS80)

LENGTH 3680m

HEIGHT GAIN 153m

APPROX CLIMB TIME 11mins

CRAGPIT HILL

ROTHBURY

This hill stutters at first – climbing, levelling, dropping – but when it does get going it hits you with a triple whammy of demanding rises that will make you cry with relief when you finally reach the moor at the top. Start on the B6341 heading east out of Rothbury and round a steep, sweeping left-hand bend up to a peak. Next there's some easy climbing before you drop down past the entrance to the Cragside Estate. Rounding Tumbleton Lake you hit the first of the three giant steps set on a constant 16%. This is the hardest of the three, and you have little time to recover before you almost immediately hit the second. Fortunately, this stretch is a fraction easier than the first; the third, following a short plateau, is a touch easier still. Once you exit the forest, you still have to reach the peak, which shouldn't be too much trouble – unless there's a stiff wind coming off the North Sea, in which case it will be hell.

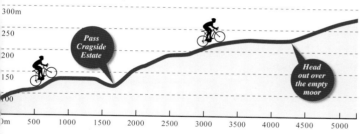

FACTFILE

WHERE Start the climb on the B6341 in Rothbury outside the Forestry Commission building. Follow the road upwards and round the left at the junction with the B6344.

GRID REF NU 089 050 (**OS**81)	
LENGTH 5250m	
HEIGHT GAIN 198m	
APPROX CLIMB TIME 18mins	

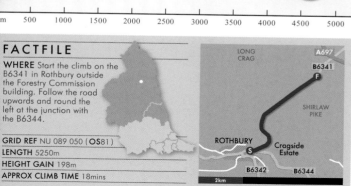

RATING
4/10

CARTER BAR

ON THE BORDER BETWEEN ENGLAND AND SCOTLAND

I resisted including this climb in previous books for the same reason I excluded the Snake Pass in Derbyshire: it gets quite busy, so is not the safest of roads. If you pick a quiet time, though, it offers a wonderful climbing experience with beautiful views across both sides of the border. In my opinion, the Scottish side, although slightly shallower, is the better of the two ascents, thanks to its collection of glorious sweeping corners. Nevertheless, back to the English side. Head north on the A68; the ups and downs end as you pass Whitelee Farm, and from here it's uphill all the way to the top. Set on a constant 6% slope, curving round the hillsides, the smooth and generously wide road creeps towards the border. It is lined with snow poles and devoid of shelter, so the higher you climb the more exposed you become, until you tip over the top to race down into Scotland.

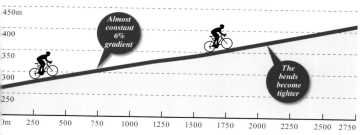

Almost constant 6% gradient

The bends become tighter

FACTFILE

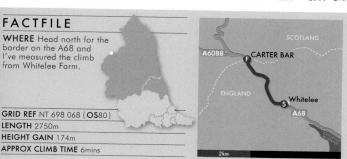

WHERE Head north for the border on the A68 and I've measured the climb from Whitelee Farm.

GRID REF NT 698 068 (**OS**80)

LENGTH 2750m

HEIGHT GAIN 174m

APPROX CLIMB TIME 6mins

CORBY'S CRAGS

EDLINGHAM

I initially came to this area to ride Lemmington Bank – a minor road that leads to the same peak from the north on a different ridge. I assumed it would offer a better riding experience as it would be quieter, but once I had tackled both roads it was clear that this was the better climb. Head away from the A697 on the B6341 towards Alnwick; there are a few fluctuations before you reach a low point round a tight left-hand bend, where the climb begins. Hard right away, the steepest slopes are at the start. A brief levelling comes between the stones walls of a small bridge. From here the climb kicks back up and snakes away into an unrelenting kilometre of slog, up to a brow where you can relax and enjoy the views out to the left. The summit lies 1,500 metres further up the road; set on a very mild incline, in the shadow of the towering crags, this last stretch shouldn't trouble the legs too much.

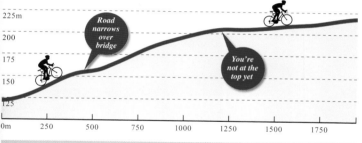

Road narrows over bridge

You're not at the top yet

FACTFILE

WHERE Simply head north-west from the A697 on the B6341 towards Alnwick.

GRID REF NU 136 108 (OS81)

LENGTH 1950m

HEIGHT GAIN 98m

APPROX CLIMB TIME 8mins

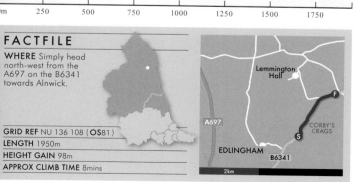

HIGH KNOWES

ALNHAM

I don't usually scan the map and head for any point where the contours are compact, but one day I did just that and stumbled upon a beauty of a road. If you're riding the National Cycle Network Route 68 and fancy heading 'off-piste' for a while – and if you like it rugged, twisting, and wild – then look no further. Turn north out of the village of Alnham, cross a cattle grid, and head into a set of four hairpin bends so tangled that the road is almost tied into a knot. After these, you climb gently across a large grassy plateau; the ever deteriorating surface bends left and right, left and right, before eventually leading you to the top of a sharp drop, from where you can see the rest of the climb laid out in all its glory. The final demanding stretch takes you high into the Cheviot Hills, and you finish just past the remains of an ancient fort. Unfortunately, it's a dead end, so you have to double back.

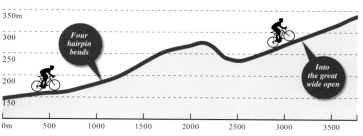

Four hairpin bends

Into the great wide open

FACTFILE

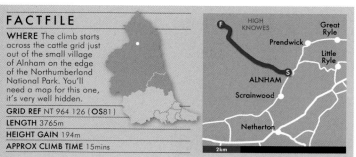

WHERE The climb starts across the cattle grid just out of the small village of Alnham on the edge of the Northumberland National Park. You'll need a map for this one, it's very well hidden.

GRID REF NT 964 126 (**OS**81)

LENGTH 3765m

HEIGHT GAIN 194m

APPROX CLIMB TIME 15mins

RATING
7/10

MIDDLETON HALL CLIMB

MIDDLETON HALL, WOOLER

OK, who likes a vicious stretch of 1-in-5? Everyone? Great, then you'll love this road hidden in the lanes south of Wooler. Although not terribly long, the killer finish to this climb packs a punch. To gain extra altitude on the ascent, I started the climb further down the valley, taking in the gentle rise up to Middleton Hall. Past the hall the road bends right and levels briefly, before turning left at the junction. After a weathered 1-in-5 sign, the road rockets up into the woods and the fun begins. The surface is rough and dirty, and you'll struggle for traction under the trees. The initially straight line hits its maximum gradient at the point where it bends left. Fighting your way round this corner you will spy the brow; keep the pressure on the pedals, search for the cleanest line, and push on up to where the steep slopes finish. You have just a handful of gentler metres to go before you reach the eventual summit.

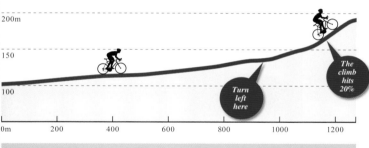

Turn left here

The climb hits 20%

FACTFILE

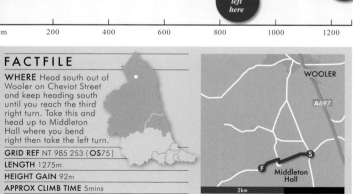

WHERE Head south out of Wooler on Cheviot Street and keep heading south until you reach the third right turn. Take this and head up to Middleton Hall where you bend right then take the left turn.

GRID REF NT 985 253 (OS75)

LENGTH 1275m

HEIGHT GAIN 92m

APPROX CLIMB TIME 5mins

WOOLER

A697

Middleton Hall

2km

RATING
5/10

LYHAM HILL

CHATTON

So stupendous were the views out over the Cheviot Hills when I rode this climb that my lack of attention to the road ahead nearly had me in the ditch. You can split the ascent neatly into two halves. The first half is pretty nondescript, although it will weaken the legs; but once past the junctions for North and South Lyham, you're ino the second half, where the landscape really comes to life. Heading up on to the moors and bending gradually left, you will see your challenge stretch out across the empty hillside. The gradient increases here, forcing you to click down a few sprockets as you round a pronounced left turn and begin the dead straight rise to the horizon. Here is where the toughest climbing lies, but the awesome views to the left will counter any discomfort in the legs. Once you reach the end of this gruelling stretch, bend right; the summit is just a few dips away.

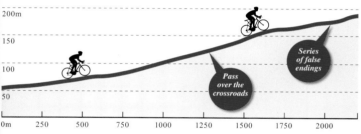

Pass over the crossroads

Series of false endings

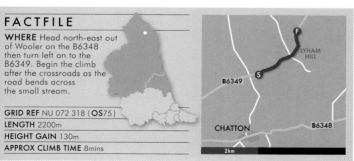

FACTFILE

WHERE Head north-east out of Wooler on the B6348 then turn left on to the B6349. Begin the climb after the crossroads as the road bends across the small stream.

GRID REF NU 072 318 (OS75)

LENGTH 2200m

HEIGHT GAIN 130m

APPROX CLIMB TIME 8mins

RATING
5/10

BARLEY HILL

KILHAM

The most satisfying climbing on this road is at the start. At the junction (on a kink in the B6351, heading towards Thornington Farm) you are immediately thrust into some solid climbing, which becomes a real challenge once you round a left-hand bend. As the road straightens you will see the distinct brow ahead, and it's a proper battle to reach it. At its steepest point, the slope hits around 17%. Once you've overcome this obstacle you will notice the gradient vanish; you bisect a farmyard on a level but extremely damaged, and more than likely mud-strewn, surface. From now on the slope is never as steep as it was at the beginning; in fact, it gets easier and easier the further you ride. There are a few kinks and bends as you rise between the fields, but nothing that constitutes a corner until you reach a lone cottage and begin the final, increasingly gentle push for the summit.

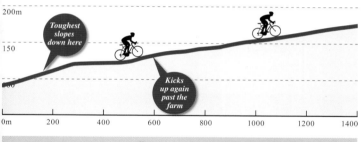

Toughest slopes down here

Kicks up again past the farm

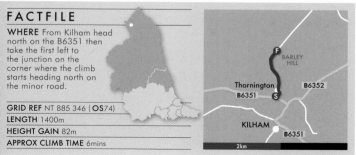

FACTFILE

WHERE From Kilham head north on the B6351 then take the first left to the junction on the corner where the climb starts heading north on the minor road.

GRID REF NT 885 346 (**OS**74)	
LENGTH 1400m	
HEIGHT GAIN 82m	
APPROX CLIMB TIME 6mins	

RIDE THEM ALL

YOU WOULD BE A FOOL NOT TO

Geographically the smallest, and certainly the least populated region in this series of books, the North-East is nonetheless home to some of the best climbs in Britain. As you will have seen on the previous pages, there's a hill to suit every rider, from long steady treks across empty moors to short sharp sprints over city centre cobbles. If you've already been filling in the checklists in the original *100 Greatest Cycling Climbs* and its sequel, *Another 100 Greatest Cycling Climbs*, then transpose those entries and get going on the rest.

TEESSIDE

Hill	Date Ridden	Time
Saltburn Road		
Skinningrove Bank		
Wilton Lane		

COUNTY DURHAM

Hill	Date Ridden	Time
South Street		
Neville Street		
Redhills Lane		
Hammer Square Bank		
Button's Bank		
Ragpath Lane		

Hedley Hill

Barley Mill Lane

Peth Bank

Iveston Bank

Goldhill Lane

Bale Hill

Yad Moss

White Edge

Middlehope Bank

Well Bank

Chapel Fell

Swinhope Head

Cuthbert's Hill

Scarsike Head

Peat Hill

Crawleyside

Unthank Bank

Wear Bank

Bollihope Common

Newbiggin Common

Miry Lane

CHECKLIST

Bail Hill		
Billy Lane		
The Stang		

NORTHUMBERLAND

Hill	Date Ridden	Time
Silverhills		
Hedley on the Hill		
Leadpipe Hill		
Prospect Hill		
Featherstone Bank		
Plenmeller Common		
Ryals Hill		
Dunterly Fell		
High Green		
Winter's Gibbet		
Cragpit Hill		
Carter Bar		
Corby's Crags		
High Knowes		
Middleton Hall Climb		
Lyham Hill		
Barley Hill		

CHECKLI

Ride them all.

BRITISH CLIMBING GUIDES ALREADY AVAILABLE